Praise for the Earth

There is no doubt that this world is in crisis. The ecological and sociological reality we're living in and must face up to is quite frankly terrifying. Yet there is hope. The authors of the *Earth Spirit* series from Moon Books show us that there are solutions to be found in ecological and eco-spiritual practices. I recommend this series to anyone who is concerned about our current situation and wants to find some hope in solutions they can practice for themselves.
Sarah Kerr, Pagan Federation President

This bold and rich *Earth Spirit* series provides vital information, perspectives, poetry and wisdom to guide and support through the complex environmental, climate and biodiversity challenges and crisis facing us all. Nothing is avoided within the wide range of author views, expertise and recommendations on eco-spirituality. I am deeply inspired by the common call, across the books, to radically change our relationship with the planet to a more respectful, mutual, spiritual and sustainable way of living; both individually and collectively. Each book offers its own particular flavour and practical offering of solutions and ways forward in these unprecedented times. Collectively the series provides an innovative, inspiring and compelling compendium of how to live, hope and act from both ancient and modern wisdoms. Whatever your views, concerns and aspirations for your life, and for the planet, you will find something of value. My life and understanding is deeply enhanced through the privilege of reading this series.
Dr Lynne Sedgmore CBE, Founder of Goddess Luminary Leadership Wheel, Executive Coach, Priestess and ex Chief Executive

In a world that is faced with such immense environmental issues, we can often feel paralysed and impotent. The *Earth Spirit* series is a welcome and inspiring antidote to fear and apathy. These books gift us with positive and inspiring visions that serve to empower and strengthen our own resolve to contribute to the healing of our planet, our communities and ourselves.

Eimear Burke, Chosen Chief of The Order of Bards, Ovates and Druids

Thanks to Moon Books and an amazing group of authors for stepping up in support of our need to address, with grace and aliveness, the ecological crises facing humanity. We must take concerted, focused, positive action on every front NOW, and this is best and most powerfully done when we base our offerings in a deep sense of spirit. White Buffalo Woman came to us 20 generations ago, reminding us of the importance of a holy perception of the world - based in Oneness, unity, honor and respect. Even as that is profound, it is also practical, giving us a baseline of power from which to give our gifts of stewardship and make our Earth walk a sacred one - for us and for All Our Relations. Walk in Beauty with these authors!

Brooke Medicine Eagle, Earthkeeper and author of *Buffalo Woman Comes Singing* and *The Last Ghost Dance*

Earth Spirit is an exciting and timely series. It has never been more important to engage with ideas that promote a positive move forward for our world. Our planet needs books like these - they offer us heartening signposts through the most challenging of times.

Philip Carr-Gomm, author of *Druid Mysteries*, *Druidcraft* and *Lessons in Magic*

Our relationship to the Mother Earth and remembering our roles as caretakers and guardians of this sacred planet is essential in weaving ourselves back into the tapestry of our own sacred nature. From the shamanic perspective, we are not separate from nature. The journey to finding solutions for the Earth will come through each person's reconnection to her heartbeat and life force.

Chandra Sun Eagle, author of *Looking Back on the Future*

This is important work as we humans face one of the greatest challenges in our collective history.

Ellen Evert Hopman, Archdruid of Tribe of the Oak and author of *A Legacy of Druids, A Druid's Herbal of Sacred Tree Medicine, The Sacred Herbs of Spring,* and other volumes

What people are saying about
Honoring the Wild

Many of us in modern Paganism are doing our best to respond to the call of the Earth in pain. A seemingly endless task, it can feel daunting, frustrating, lonely, depressingly insurmountable. This little book says, "keep going", as if Irisanya and the intersectional group of writers whose voices she shares have taken your hands to march beside you. The stories and rituals herein are full of grief, and fury, and love, but most of all they are empowering and uplifting, and they show what we – as a community and as individuals – can do, and some of the many parts we can play. I am not a member of the Reclaiming tradition, but I came away feeling proud, heartened and inspired by a group that centres activism as one of its core tenets. This healing, this gentle but resolute strength, is the kind of magick our world needs at this moment.

Katrina Townsend, author of *The Anti-consumerist Druid*

Most pagans already are, in some way, doing what they can to help the planet. *Earth Spirit: Honoring the Wild* is a collection of voices from the Reclaiming witchcraft tradition, showing the range of their achievements. It is one of the most inspiring books about environmental activism I have read. As author Irisanya Moon writes: 'Activism shows up in many ways, in many forms.' Not everyone can go on long marches or stand for hours in protest, although many do. If you reuse and recycle, if you do magic to protect wildlife, if you write poetry to raise awareness – you are still an activist. If you are looking for ideas about what more you can do, read this book.

Lucya Starza, author of Pagan Portals titles on *Candle Magic, Poppets and Magical Dolls, Guided Visualisations,* and *Scrying*

Earth Spirit
Honoring the Wild

Reclaiming Witchcraft and
Environmental Activism

Earth Spirit
Honoring the Wild

Reclaiming Witchcraft and
Environmental Activism

Irisanya Moon

MOON
BOOKS
Winchester, UK
Washington, USA

JOHN HUNT PUBLISHING

First published by Moon Books, 2023
Moon Books is an imprint of John Hunt Publishing Ltd., No. 3 East Street, Alresford
Hampshire SO24 9EE, UK
office@jhpbooks.net
www.johnhuntpublishing.com
www.moon-books.net

For distributor details and how to order please visit the 'Ordering' section on our website.

ISBN: 978 1 78904 961 9
978 1 78904 962 6 (ebook)
Library of Congress Control Number: 2022930135

A CIP catalogue record for this book is available from the British Library.

Design: Matthew Greenfield

UK: Printed and bound by CPI Group (UK) Ltd, Croydon, CR0 4YY
Printed in North America by CPI GPS partners

We operate a distinctive and ethical publishing philosophy in
all areas of our business, from our global network of authors to
production and worldwide distribution.

Contents

Acknowledgements & Dedication

There are many people to thank for their help in creating this book. Not only do I thank my publisher for reaching out with this idea and for the folks who wrote pieces to add to this compilation, but I also thank the activists of before, now, and the future.

It is upon their shoulders I stand and see the ongoing impact of action and magick.

While there is no hierarchy in activism for me, there is one name to which I want to dedicate this book: Rose May Dance.

Rose was one of my first teachers at California Witchcamp in 2008. Her silliness and her creativity inspire me to this date.

What I didn't know at the time was that she and I were from the same Ohio city. I also didn't know she was an activist, someone who trained health counselors and outreach workers in 'how to reach the hard to reach.' Rose was a vital part of the harm reduction movement that led to the inception of the needle exchange program (Prevention Point) in San Francisco, California.

Rose also helped to found Reclaiming Witchcraft, as an activist for peace, as well as social and environmental justice. She helped create hundreds of rituals and participated in numerous actions in support of environmental causes, many of these actions are listed in this book.

Rose May Dance died on December 31, 2021. To her, I dedicate this book.

Introduction

"The Diablo blockade was an initiation; a journey through fear, a descent into the dark, and a return with knowledge and empowerment from within; a death and rebirth that began with a stripping process and promises something at the end." – Starhawk, *Dreaming the Dark*

This is a short and impossible book. It is an all-too-brief compilation of voices that have been in Reclaiming. It is a collection of snapshots – where bodies have been. Where ritual existed and can exist next. The work of activism is ongoing, imperfect, and an invitation to continue. To change and to adjust to the emerging needs, the insistent call from Earth. The time is always right now.

Activism shows up in many ways, in many forms, and sometimes it shows up, burns out, and disappears. Or returns, in another form. Sometimes activism is less of being in the crowd and more like holding the edges. Sometimes activism is loud. Sometimes it is quiet. Sometimes it is both and beyond. My hope is to bring to light the way Reclaiming Witches and magick makers honor (and honour) the wild.

I am certain this is incomplete. I am certain I will forget or confuse a fact. For that, I take accountability. The words of the writers are as close to their original offerings as possible. The only words that have been adjusted are for clarity and grammar/spelling/punctuation. The pieces are placed in an order that originally flowed from what was offered, from story to practice to magick and beyond. It is not linear. It is not created with any sense of one piece being more or less important than the next. All of these pieces were given of the heart.

What you will want to know is that I wanted to show the reader, Reclaiming or not, what activism looks like from the inside. While the outside and the pictures and the outcomes and the victories and the disappointments are many, the emotions are just as mighty and many. The 'why' has always been more valuable than the 'how' to me. Because when you are clear on the direction, you will find a way to get there. When your heart is the compass, the journey reveals itself.

The Earth is hurting. Witches are healers. May the work continue. Blessed be the hands and hearts of each being.

Principles of Unity[1]

Author Note: In my previous book, "Pagan Portals – Reclaiming Witchcraft," Reclaiming was in the process of discussing how the Principles of Unity (POU) might need to change to better care for and support BIPOC humans in the tradition. At Dandelion 2019, a global gathering of Reclaiming Witches, the POU did change. I had already written that book before the changes were made, so the following POU is the most current version as of 2021. It will likely change again. It is a living document.

"My law is love unto all beings..." – from The Charge of the Goddess by Doreen Valiente

The values of the Reclaiming tradition stem from our understanding that the earth is alive and all of life is sacred and interconnected. We see the Goddess as immanent in the earth's cycles of birth, growth, death, decay and regeneration. Our practice arises from a deep, spiritual commitment to the earth, to healing and to the linking of magic with political action.

Each of us embodies the divine. Our ultimate spiritual authority is within, and we need no other person to interpret the sacred to us. We foster the questioning attitude, and honor intellectual, spiritual and creative freedom.

We are an evolving, dynamic tradition and proudly call ourselves Witches. Our diverse practices and experiences of the divine weave a tapestry of many different threads. We include those who honor Mysterious Ones, Goddesses, and Gods of myriad expressions, genders, and states of being, remembering that mystery goes beyond form. Our community rituals are participatory and ecstatic, celebrating the cycles of the seasons and our lives, and raising energy for personal, collective and earth healing.

We know that everyone can do the life-changing, world-renewing work of magic, the art of changing consciousness at will. We strive to teach and practice in ways that foster personal and collective empowerment, to model shared power and to open leadership roles to all. We make decisions by consensus, and balance individual autonomy with social responsibility.

Our tradition honors the wild, and calls for service to the earth and the community. We work in diverse ways, including nonviolent direct action, for all forms of justice: environmental, social, political, racial, gender and economic. We are an anti-racist tradition that strives to uplift and center BIPOC voices (Black, Indigenous, People of Color). Our feminism includes a radical analysis of power, seeing all systems of oppression as interrelated, rooted in structures of domination and control.

We welcome all genders, all gender histories, all races, all ages and sexual orientations and all those differences of life situation, background, and ability that increase our diversity. We strive to make our public rituals and events accessible and safe. We try to balance the need to be justly compensated for our labor with our commitment to make our work available to people of all economic levels.

All living beings are worthy of respect. All are supported by the sacred elements of air, fire, water and earth. We work to create and sustain communities and cultures that embody our values, that can help to heal the wounds of the earth and her peoples, and that can sustain us and nurture future generations.

Reclaiming Principles of Unity – consensed by the Reclaiming Collective in 1997. Updated by consensus at the BIRCH council meeting of Dandelion Gathering 5 in 2012 and at the BIRCH Council meeting in January 2021.

Note

1. https://reclaimingcollective.wordpress.com/principles-of-unity/ (accessed 2021)

An Activism Timeline

If a New Way is Possible
Let it come to us
Like ripe fruit falls.
—David Samas

With the help of George Franklin and many voices in Reclaiming via an email conversation, I am able to offer this timeline. Of course, not everyone is on email groups or lists. Not everyone was able to collaborate. And memories can sometimes conflict. And there are so many stories that could be told. I tried to include them all. I'm sure there are missing pieces. I'm sure there are some who might think things happened in another year...

As a constantly evolving tradition that tells stories and has had many Witches come and go, this timeline is as complete as it can be, with the voices that know more than me. When we can all sit by the campfire again, let us all share the stories that have not made it to these pages.

So, here is an annotated timeline of environmental and other direct actions that Reclaiming folks have been part of in some form. It should be said that anti-nuclear actions were always environmentally focused. Handbooks created for specific actions included documentation of environmental and social impacts of nuclear power and weapons and militarism and the arms industry in general.

Many actions and handbooks emphasized "environmental racism," the disproportionate impact on poor communities and People of Color, who often stand closest to the dangers and impacts of nukes, militarism, and energy production.

Handbooks from the 1980s actions: DirectAction.org/handbooks

Timeline

1976 / Seabrook, NH Anti-nuclear power actions that sparked a decade of anti-nuke activism, including folks later involved in East Coast witchcamps and the Clamshell Alliance.

1979 / Diablo Canyon, CA First major anti-nuclear power action on the West Coast. Early proto-Reclaiming affinity groups took part. Many folks had their first civil disobedience arrest. Abalone Alliance.

1979 / SF Spiral Dance Following this action, the book *The Spiral Dance* and the first Spiral Dance ritual were held at Samhain that year.

1980s / NorCal Annual protests of the ultra-privileged Bohemian Club which meets each Summer in Northern CA. Vigils, actions, activists floating down Russian River through the Boho site.

1980s/1990s / Headwaters Forest Reserve, Fortuna, CA Forest defense actions, including rally, march, and spiral dance with hundreds of people under a double rainbow.

1981 / Diablo Canyon, CA Largest anti-nuke action to date, involving 2000 arrests. Many Reclaiming people involved.

1982 / Livermore, CA First large-scale anti-nuclear weapons direct action, with 1400 arrests and 5000 participating. This action set off a string of protests at Livermore Weapons Lab, Vandenberg Air Force Base, and in downtown San Francisco. Actions at Livermore and Site 300 continued for years.

1983 (Jan-June) / CA Major civil disobedience occupations of Vandenberg Air Force base, in protest of testing of new long-range missiles. About 1000 arrests.

1983 (June) / Livermore, CA Second large-scale anti-nuclear weapons direct action, with 1100 arrests and 5000 participating. 7-10 day jail sentences. Major Matrix affinity group and Change of Heart Cluster action (many Pagans in both). Solstice ritual and Gay Pride march in jail.

1983 / San Francisco, CA Anti-corporate tour sponsored by Abalone Alliance (Anti-nuke power)

1983 / Concord, CA First "solidarity" action, joining Central America support groups to protest shipments of US arms to repressive Central American regimes. Actions at Concord NWS continued for years.

1984 (July) / San Francisco, CA War Chest Tours during Democratic Convention, protesting corporate links to nukes, war, and environmental degradation. "War Chest Tours" continued for several years, and occasionally recurred in later years. Solstice in the Streets used this same "roving corporate visits" model.

1984 (Sept) / Livermore, CA Enola Gay affinity group did a ritual at Livermore Lab, poured blood and chanted: "The blood of gay men is sacred." One of the first actions demanding "Money for AIDS, Not for War."

1985 / Livermore, CA Hiroshima/Nagasaki actions took place many years. 1985 was a major action, 40th anniversary of the bombings.

1987 (June) / Concord, CA One of numerous actions at Concord Naval Weapons Station, joining solidarity groups to protest arms shipments to Central America.

1988 (Nov) / SF Two Reclaiming witches launched one of the first needle exchange interventions with street-based injection drug users in San Francisco's Tenderloin District, soon joined by others. The intervention began November 2, 1988, Day of the Dead.

1987-89 / Nevada Test Site Largest of a decade of mass direct actions opposing nuclear testing and supporting the claims of the Western Shoshone in the area. About 4000 people total were arrested in these two years alone. Reclaiming affinity groups took part in these actions and the encampments that took root on federal land adjacent to the test site.

1991 / Anti-War Actions Reclaiming folks around the network took part in protests, vigils, and other activism in opposition to the 1991 Gulf War. Many were arrested in direct actions, and street theater was a strong part of Reclaiming involvement in the Bay Area.

1991-95 / Berkeley, CA Peoples Park defense and birth of East Bay Food Not Bombs, both involving Reclaiming folks.

1992 Rodney King Riots Spontaneous protests and riots after the trial of the police who beat Rodney King. First actual riots in some cities in a decade or more, providing education for some activists.

1993 / Clayoquot Sound, BC Blockade at Clayoquot Sound on Vancouver Island, BC, Canada to stop the logging of an old growth forest.

1995 / SF Stolen Lives One of the early manifestations of what grew into the Black Lives Matter movement. Reclaiming folks co-sponsored a vigil near a major tourist site in downtown San Francisco, drawing attention to police killings of young People of Color.

1999 / Seattle WTO Dozens of activists from around the Reclaiming network converged as the Pagan Cluster in Seattle in late 1999 for what proved to be generation-defining protests against corporate globalization. Joined ranks with unions and people from many other movements, the raucous week of protests helped spark a decade of anti-globalization actions around the world.

2000s / Various Actions at the biennial "BIO" corporate conferences in the 2000s – in St Louis (2002-3), SF (2004), Boston (2000), and other cities. Reclaiming folks anchored 2004 SF convergence center.

2001 / NYC Post-911 actions.

2001 (Apr) / Quebec City WTO/IMF Living River born, an activist group that still exists today.

2001 (Oct) / Ottawa IMF/World Bank

2002 (Feb) / NYC World Economic Forum Led a spiral dance in Grand Central and a huge Brigid ritual in Washington Square.

2002 (Apr) / DC IMF-World Bank Actions March for Palestine. Early anti-war marches.

2002 (June) / Calgary G8 Meetings

2002 (Sept) / DC IMF-World Bank Actions anti-war marches begin. Mass arrest of nearly the entire Pagan Cluster.

2002 (Fall) / Various Anti-War actions in many locales.

2003 (Jan-Mar) / Major anti-war mobilizations in DC, SF, NYC and many other cities.

2003 (June) / Sacto Environmental Action Major militarist/ police presence. Mud People arrested.

2003 / Cancun TWO Meetings Biggest gathering yet of Pagan Cluster activists. rented house for about 30 people for the month.

2003 (Oct) / Miami FTAA Meetings Rented three houses to hold everyone; several folks were pepper sprayed and rubber bulleted by police.

2003 (Fall) / Various Anti-war actions in various cities, major mobilization in DC in Oct.

2004 / Texas First Dandelion Reclaiming gathering – visioning gathering of activists & organizers, Pagan Cluster rituals.

2004 (April) / Washington DC Pagan Cluster contingent for the March for Women's Lives and IMF protests.

2004 (June) / Brunswick G8 meetings Brunswick, GA Police outnumbered activists.

2004 (Aug) / NYC Republican Convention Amazing actions with Pagan Cluster folks anchoring pieces of this mobilization.

2005 (June) / Texas Camp Casey

2005 (Aug) / New Orleans Hurricane Katrina Initially about 20 Pagan Cluster activists helped set up emergency infrastructure throughout the 9th & 7th wards & shuttle supplies out to rural communities.

2006 / Grants Pass, OR Forest defense action at The Biscuit after the first Free Activist Witchcamp.

2008 (Sept) / St Paul Republican Convention Actions

2009 (Sept) / Pittsburgh G20 meetings Mean police and LRAD (sound cannon) is used.

2009-10 / New Mexico Think Outside the Bomb Tour

2011 / Solstice in Streets Celebratory pro-Earth action in SF Organized by Teen Earth Magic.

2011 / Everywhere Occupy! Reclaiming folks involved in organizing, civil disobedience, and living at camps in numerous cities. Make Banks Pay protests in SF.

2012 (Aug) / Charlotte Democratic Convention March and actions.

2013-15 /Concord, CA Chevron actions addressing environmental racism. Lots of street theater, civil disobedience.

2014 / Various Black Lives Matter Major protests in late 2014 in various cities.

2014 / NYC Pagan Cluster contingent at the NYC Peoples Climate March as well as collaborative projects for regenerative culture.

2016 / Foley Square NYC Reclaiming Anti-Trump Marches and rallies.

2017 / Women's March

2017 (April) / Washington DC Peoples' Climate March

2017 / SF Solidarity actions and marches in opposition to the Dakota Access Pipeline in SF and New York City.

2019 / SF Environmental street festival Shut down 10 blocks of the Financial District. Monthly actions in SF and other cities sponsored by Sunflower Movement, Extinction Rebellion, etc.

Additional points of interest and note:

- Reclaiming groups were part of the successful movement to ban fracking in New York State (2009-2014), focusing on ensuring the inclusion of Haudenosaunee perspectives and leaders, as well as the We Are Seneca Lake blockade of the massive expansion of Crestwood's fracked gas storage facility in leaking salt caverns under Seneca Lake (2014-2015).
- After the bombing of Judi Bari and Darryl Cherney, Reclaiming activists (Modoc, Max, and Mary Liz) made an organizing video to ensure the organizing and actions would continue that summer. Many groups and affinity groups jumped into action to be sure forest defense would not be slowed down, obviously the intention of the bombing.

As you've no doubt noticed, many of the actions above are not describing environmental goals. The call to action in all of these settings is interwoven. Calling attention to those in power who have histories of broken promises or overall ignorance of environmental issues is part of the activist history. The calls for change continue. The story continues.

Story

Deep Witnessing: Love and Rage-Sweat and Tears
Kim Chilvers

Connecting with Place and Connecting with the Earth

Changing consciousness at will. What happens between the worlds changes the worlds. We say magic changes the world, but when doing activism how much do we mean this? I have done my share of street activism and everything from letter writing to ritual, sitting-in to blockading for social justice and environmental awareness, but the environmental activism that has had the biggest impact on my life has been a silent connection with our living planet.

My deepest experiences with magical activism have been in very deep witnessing; opening up to the emotions, the energy and the spirits of the action, place, or ritual being enacted. I have had the pleasure of two particularly life-changing experiences of this sort of magical activism.

The first was a backcountry action in the Headwaters old growth redwood forest in 1997. The second was my time in the Red Rebel Brigade with SF Bay Area Extinction Rebellion in 2019.

Three related magical practices, common in Reclaiming, are among the tools which have allowed and trained me to sense energy, to watch, to witness, to connect, and to interact in a deeper way to the beings, the land, the spirits of place, and the Earth herself. The first of these is dropped and open attention, the second is anchoring, and the third is aspecting.

Dropped and open attention is a way to feel energy and sense surroundings using your emotions and five senses in a more open and expansive manner. The process is to draw one's focus into a small ball in your head, or on top of your crown chakra, then pull in down inside your body to your heart, core, or sex, then expand the ball of awareness to the edges of your physical body, then to the edges of your aura and even beyond.

Anchoring is taking dropped and open attention to a larger space, opening the space of awareness to a room or larger area. This includes incorporating the beings in that space and holding it in silent stillness and witnessing deeply for anywhere from a few minutes to a couple of hours in a deep trance state. This is usually used for large rituals, such as the Spiral Dance, in order to "watch," which assists in holding, grounding, or containing the energetic flow as well as providing a very deep feeling, hearing, or observation.

Aspecting is a lighter level of trance possession where the spirit of a deity, for example, comes through a person while that person's awareness is also still present. Anchoring uses the same tool of managing awareness, but instead of observing surroundings in a different way it involves the experience of something coming through and temporarily merging with one's personal awareness.

In 1997 a large group of Reclaiming witches gathered, camped, rallied, marched, and participated in days of actions supporting forest protection to save the old growth redwood forest of the Headwaters area in Humboldt County in Northwestern California. A smaller group of 26 of us decided to do a back country hike as a magical action in the heart of the old growth forest. This involved sneaking into privately owned land slated for logging, in the middle of the night, and hiking with Earth First guides deep in the forest. The next day, we did a ritual connecting, experiencing, and offering what we could for protection, then hiking out that evening after spending approximately 24 hours in forest rarely seen or touched by humans. Hiking late into the night and sleeping only a couple of hours on the forest floor, open to the canopy and sky, set the stage for the depth of the work the next day. In the morning we hiked to a beautiful natural spring where we created sacred space and spent time in silent open attention communing with the land and trees. This depth of connection, of feeling, of communicating with the spirits of the land, the trees, the ferns, the moss, and the mycorrhizal fungi (which live in the root systems of redwoods and allows them to communicate with each other) was life changing for many of us. "Nothing will ever be the same" wrote Toni Savage in the 1997 Reclaiming Quarterly edition focusing on this action.

Nearly six months later some of us aspected redwood trees for a ritual at Pantheacon, which provided the "forest" for a ritual re-enacting this action in a ritual in a convention hotel. The trees don't "speak" through us like deities do; even translated through our filters they do not speak English. My experience is that they communicate energetically, which can barely be translated to words. In this case aspecting was used as a deeper form of ritual theater, forming a deeper connection to a being or archetype, not just to pretend or act the role. In Reclaiming, magical tradition often uses aspecting in this way.

More recently, I began doing work with Extinction Rebellion (XR), being drawn to the emotionally present and theatrical nature of their actions. Seeing activism as magic and magic as activism, I felt this was a fit for me. I was honored to be able to do several actions as part of the SF Bay Area Red Rebel Troup. The Red Rebels were started by Doug Fransesco, a performance artist in Bristol, England, whose videos of the performances, actions, and "rituals" of the Red Rebels went viral, and other Red Rebel groups continue to move in silence through natural and urban settings, holding the love, rage, grief, and hope we all feel as manifested in the red of all of our blood. Although there were other witches in the bay area Troup, this was not a Reclaiming or even pagan action, yet it was clearly magical as a way of embodiment of the grief and interconnection of all beings for the harm we as humans are doing to the earth. I participated in this movable sacred space and in dropped and open attention to "feel" the connection to the planet, and often moved into anchoring when still for long periods or aspecting while interacting with the crowds. Because all of our work is socially complicated, the Bay Area Red Rebel Troup decided to no longer "wear red" in that role in actions to honor our Native American allies and the Red Dress Movement.

Actions, stopping destruction, and drawing attention to injustices are very important in our work to make the world a better place and to save our planet. Through these and other experiences, I believe using our magical skills more deeply to feel, see, and connect is activism and the kind of activism we as witches, especially Reclaiming witches, are uniquely skilled in. At the very least, this type of action symbolically represents grief and connection, and may change the participants who can then carry it into our human communities. At most, it creates real energetic shift, healing, and protective change for ourselves and the Earth.

The Saving of Twin Lakes
Randy Ellen Blaustein

"The Twin Lakes Preserve, located on Old Mill Road in Wantagh, is dedicated to the understanding, preservation and enjoyment of Long Island's natural environment. The 58-acre preserve features five freshwater ponds and extensive sections of freshwater wetlands and transitional stage woodlands. In its picturesque and serene setting, residents may partake of such outdoor activities as bird watching, sports fishing or hiking and exploring along a trail system. The preserve also serves as a nature study area for those who wish to expand their knowledge of the environment." – from the Town of Hempstead's website https://hempsteadny.gov/preserves-and-nature-areas/twin-lakes-preserve

This is a story of perseverance and tenacity. This is a story of grassroots organizing at its finest! This is a story that took place in 1979; there was no internet, no cell phones. There was posting flyers on telephone poles and posters in store windows; handing flyers out on the street; going door-to-door with petitions; making phone calls; holding meetings in the library after hours. This is also a story about my mother, Alice Blaustein's environmental activism.

I grew up in a neighborhood on Long Island, on the border of North Bellmore and Wantagh. Our residence was in North Bellmore; my two siblings and myself went to public school there. But our mailing address and zip code was Wantagh. About a half a mile from our house was Twin Lakes; a lovely forested area, with lakes, located behind Forest Lake Elementary School, in Wantagh.

I was living in Massachusetts; during the summer of 1979, I went back to Long Island to visit my birth family. My mother taught at the, now defunct Long Island Developmental Center, an institution that housed people of all ages with intellectual and developmental disabilities. She had summers off, and that summer fiercely dove head first into helping save Twin Lakes; most of my visit was spent learning about what that entailed.

All I have to tell her story is my memories and a copy of an article written for the Wantagh local newspaper, by Joan Kern, the woman who led the battle to save the lakes. There is no history to be found anywhere on the internet of how Twin Lakes was once in jeopardy of being demolished.

Twin Lakes was my Mom's place of solace. Whenever she needed to take space for herself, she would take our Yellow Lab, Rex for a walk to this tranquil wooded area, and sit by the water. One day, she saw an article in the paper stating that the forest and lakes property were in danger of being bought by a land developer who had built a shopping mall, and had big plans for condos and a shopping center. By some fluke, the land was owned by the City of New York, and due to unpaid back taxes, was being auctioned off. My Mom immediately called the phone number to help save Nassau's watersheds from the NYC public auction.

Alice became a volunteer extraordinaire! She offered to provide refreshments before meeting the other people involved, set up the library table, dispensed petitions, delivered posters, made numerous phone calls, put the raffles together, and did anything else that was needed.

This little grassroots group, made up of concerned citizens, called in the National Environmental Protection Agency, who after surveying the land, declared the area a natural habitat that should not be disturbed. They managed to get top level politicians on their side who advocated for their cause; had parents and teachers at the elementary school help obtain signatures on the petition; presented the petitions with thousands of signatures at a Mineola Board of Supervisors meeting. Their efforts paid off! The land developer could not believe he was defeated by this small group of concerned citizens!

The Town of Hempstead Department of Conservation and Waterways maintains this beautiful property to this day; they named it Twin Lakes Preserve. The sign on a gate entrance states: "Preserved by The Town of Hempstead Department of Conservation and Waterways to protect and enrich the environment." I am proud that my Mom was instrumental in the battle to keep this preserve protected. I imagine the history known to the people involved has been passed down orally. I don't know of any other accounts that have been written down.

Untitled
Shannon Rose Raison

I dreamt I was on a bus travelling to a witchcamp on the outskirts of an urban center. Reclaiming elders walked the aisles and pointed out the sites. There were elaborate domed greenhouses protected in magical rainbow cloaks of invisibility. Classes of dance warriors were training in acts of artful, expressive defense and action. It was beautiful, hopeful, and inspiring, and yet it was not mine to engage in or write about. When I got off the bus, I ended up late to the lunch table with nothing left for me to eat.

As I write this old growth forests on Pacheedaht and Ditidaht territories about an hour's drive to the west of me are being logged as hundreds of land defenders actively try to stop them. Over 150 people have been arrested. Many of those arrested are indigenous youth who have been targeted not only by the RCMP, but also by residents and loggers in the local logging town where the blockaders seek their supplies and down-time.

As I sat with writing this piece and this way too familiar story unfolding around me a different future vision arose before me. A future vision in which Reclaiming continues to work towards embodying decolonization in all that we do but especially in our environmental activism, much of which takes place on stolen land. I believe this is something we struggle with as a community. I know many of us want to do this better. I know we have caused harm. I think not continuing to grapple with it deeply perpetuates that harm.

I am an uninvited white settler of Irish, Polish, English, and German descent living on Quw'utsun territories on what is colonially known as Vancouver Island in B.C. From this place I want to ask us as Reclaiming witches. What does it mean to be witches doing magic on stolen land? What does it mean to be witches of mixed ancestral backgrounds, most displaced, displacees, and displacers, from their own ancestral lands? How does our magical activism not only acknowledge but also help to dismantle these systems?

I don't have all the answers but I have a desire to see a future in Reclaiming where indigenous sovereignty is centered. Where we explore how our own environmental activism can support Land Back and indigenous voices. It is a common practice in decoloniality-informed activist circles to use white bodies as a front-line defense to protect BIPOC activists who are more likely to be harmed and targeted. Where I live indigenous led environmental actions often centre spiritual and ancestral practices. I want to see a future where we use Reclaiming ritual technology (when asked for) to support these practices. I want to see those of us that are white in Reclaiming use our magical bodies as a front-line defense for indigenous land defenders.

I also have inspiration.

The first year I landed on the territories where I currently live, we held a Beltane ritual where we invited some local Elders that we had relationships with. Stories were shared from different ancestries; the maypole was danced to the drumming and Coast Salish songs of one of these Elders. The following Fall at our Samhain ritual we planned to burn this maypole at the centre of our fire.

The morning of the Samhain ritual a local teaching was shared with us from one of the Quw'utsun Elders who had been at the Beltane ritual. The details of this teaching are not mine to share, but to illustrate the point I will share simply that part of this involved creating a table-like structure out of wood that would be lit on fire and serve as the vessel to deliver to the offerings we had planned for the ancestors of the land.

Somehow creating this structure with the phallic maypole in the middle of the 'table' seemed deeply wrong. We were unable to arrive at anything that felt just right. Then as the fire tenders started to make steps towards building the fire in-the-moment inspiration struck. We made the somewhat heart-wrenching decision to cut the maypole. We cut through the ribbons, magic, and intentions of our Beltane ritual and used them to create the four foundational pieces of the table-like structure to carry the offerings for Quw'utsun ancestors of the lands.

This decision was hard to make. Many of us energetically cringed as the maypole was sawed into pieces. Watching something we had put so much magic and vision into transforming into something we could not have predicted felt deeply uncomfortable, wrong even in its rightness. As far as I can tell this is what decolonial magic feels like.

It's the transformation of long-held beliefs, customs, practices, and rituals. It's listening, and then unlearning, and then adapting, and then doing it all over again. It's deeply uncomfortable and even painful. It calls us to question things we did not realize were questionable. It is many, many things as the pure multiplicity of it counteracts the uniformity inherent in colonialism. It is more than I or anyone alone can speak to or dream into being. It is collective, it is expansive.

This is the future I want to see in Reclaiming and in how we approach environmental activism. It is one I believe we are stumbling towards as our community continues to grow and include and support voices with different experiences around colonization, relationship to land, and activism. I see its possibility reflected in the recent changes made to the Principles of Unity. I believe it is possible and I also see it as deeply challenging. And so I bring us this question as a community: Can the maypole become the table upon which the indigenous ancestors and descendants of the lands we hope to save are fed?

Practice

Disabled, Pagan ... and Green?
Sylvia Rose

Sometimes being disabled seems enough of a life challenge to be getting on with. Much as you love the natural world, getting out into it at all might be an achievement for you, let alone going out and campaigning to save it. Sometimes self-care needs to come first, whether we like it or not. So can we also be "green"?

As I see it, green is as much an attitude as a prescriptive set of actions, and at its best it stems not from guilt but from love. No I shouldn't really be buying these green beans flown in from Kenya in the middle of winter, but I really fancy them. But, the thought of all those unnecessary carbon emissions hurts, and anyway I'd rather that super-fresh first of the season purple sprouting broccoli grown locally.

It seems to me that we have inherited, whether we like it or not, a very long Judeo-Christian tradition that virtue means personal deprivation, even when our lives are deprived enough already. The world will be a better place if I deprive myself of chocolate for Lent. Will it? Only if I then donate the money I've saved to charity. So much of the current rhetoric around environmentalism is about making personal life changes. But actually, if I never took a flight again in my life, the climate would still be heading for catastrophe. Even if I guilt-tripped all my friends into doing likewise, it still wouldn't make enough difference. The most frequent flyers aren't we tourists, they're business people, politicians, people caught in a system predicated on flying.

If I never used a single-use plastic bottle or straw again, the ocean would still be clogged with plastic, because 60% of it is from damaged or discarded fishing gear. And a large portion of the rest comes as outflow from only ten rivers, mostly in the developing world, where there is a severe lack of organised rubbish collection so the river does the job instead. So if we want change, it is the systems that need change more than our individual consumer habits.

You know all the cardboard food packaging that comes with plastic 'viewing windows' built in? Because I'm obstinate and a little obsessive, I tear out the plastic each time so it can go in the landfill bin while the cardboard goes in the recycling. But even as I'm doing it, I'm wondering how many other people bother. Wouldn't it be better if we had just rules against mixed-material packaging? And is the government about to introduce them, in the face of inevitable hostility from the business community, some of whom contribute generously to Party funds? Not unless we make them.

This can happen. Since that one programme by David Attenborough, since the outcry of caring about the ocean that followed, cafe chains are suddenly selling reusable cups, the government is promising returnable bottle schemes, plastic packaging is being reduced, things are changing. Because enough people have shown that they care. Because sometimes where you spend your money has the greatest impact in driving change.

So, for me, being green isn't about personal deprivation. Sure, it's about living simply, avoiding unnecessary consumption, not buying crap just to cheer myself up. But it's more about opening my heart, staying in touch with caring for our world even when it gets so painful. It's about every petition you've signed and shared, every Facebook meme you've passed on of what's going right, as well as what's going wrong. Every conversation you've had that goes, isn't the weather fabulous right now? Yes, but the swallows shouldn't really be here yet, it's only February, there are not enough insects around for them, this is not good.

And it's being visible, as and when you can. Wear your activist t-shirts. Forward events to someone who might actually be able to attend. Even consider whether you could get to one yourself.

(Sometimes I look at an action that mainly involves lying in the road and think, even I could do that! But I probably couldn't also do all the energy-expenditure that's presumably involved in getting arrested afterwards too.) Many protest marches now are, following campaigning from disabled people to be included too, making a safe space at the front for people with mobility difficulties, wheelchairs, children and pushchairs etc. Sometimes there's even a bus for us all to head the march. It's worth asking. Our voices count too. Being disabled and being green is not an either/or. It's a both/and. Though maybe with a little more creativity and thought.

So, being green. It's in our hearts, in our love of the Earth. In our thoughtfulness about our purchasing choices. In our conversations. In our social media sharing. In our donations to green charities. It's in every time we can afford to buy organic, to buy from our local market, every time we vote with our wallets. It's in every time we feed the birds.

And of course it's in our rituals, our magic, our conversations with our Godds as well. But that's another story...

Witch, Yes. Environmental Activist? No.
Georgie Craig

This was hard for me to write. I am not an ecological activist.

So why am I writing this? Because I believe I should stop hiding in the non-activist-closet side of the Reclaiming house, And I should stop pretending that I was there. I mean as people get old, they forget who actually showed up.

I do still feel a lot of guilt for not tromping through the Redwood forest and chaining myself to a tree. I feel bad that I didn't and don't go to demonstrations or marches or any large group protests. I have White privilege. I'm an older, middle-class woman. That means I can offer myself as protection, a shield. I can talk to those in power because they think I'm powerless. They don't see me as the other, as a threat. Yet, I don't go.

And it's really not that I'm too old to tromp through the forest without my poles these days. Though realistically unless someone has the ability to carry me over trees, I am too old. The truth is even when I was younger, and scrambling out of bars and clubs on 4-inch heels was part of my repertoire, I would freeze at the suggestion of ecological activism.

A little background. I was raised in Oakland during the 60s. My older siblings were anti-war protestors but my father was an Oakland police officer. He was an alcoholic who, after drinking, turned into a violent, rage-fueled abuser.

I wasn't often the target for his anger. But I watched the beatings and heard the yelling. I heard the anger and betrayal my father felt because his children dared to think differently. I promised myself I wouldn't draw that kind of anger to me. I became a people pleasing co-dependent.

And now, after finding Reclaiming and becoming part of the weft and weave of this tradition, I am straining for the self-acceptance that I can't tread the activist path. To be crystal, maybe quartz crystal, clear, no one is asking me too. I'm putting the pressure on myself. I have ecological activism FOMO. And when I occasionally speak of joining some protest or another, those who know me best, as in Rose May Dance asks the somewhat embarrassing question to me: "What good would you be at a protest? We don't need to have to take care of you too."

What I've realized as I'm becoming my Crone self is: I have the privilege to choose another path.

So, I decided to do what I could do. Learn more, so I could teach this tradition and support the teachers who are out there in public, disseminating the knowledge that will enable Reclaiming to continue long after I set sail for the Island of Apples.

Create opportunities for public rituals to bring more folks into this living tradition. Go to witchcamps to meet other Witches from far flung places so I can learn more about what others are facing. Volunteer at Reclaiming's Samhain fundraiser,

The Spiral Dance, to support and further this tradition's work.

And provide material support to those who are putting themselves on the front lines so they know they'll be taken care of. One thing among many I love about Reclaiming is wherever you fall on any spectrum you will find those who understand, support, and love you no matter what.

Sprinkling Magic in the Mundane
BrightFlame

Padding through the woods naked, my toes sink into rich dark soil, and I inhale the sweet mineral scent of the forest floor as if I'm a coyote with nostrils flared. A breast-high gray boulder invites me to lean, and I shiver against its cool smoothness, reading the pale lichen patterns on its surface like a map. So many delights, so much beauty, so much information once I open to the language of Nature. I stick my nose into brown hemlock bark, and an ant crawls across my forehead, detoured from its mission. In dappled sunlight filtered through leaves, among velvet moss and feathery fern, I fall in love with the land again.

Forest and Ocean are sacred. They are my kin.

Such is the feeling I aim to conjure through my writing, teaching, and priestexxing. Wouldn't we be closer to a just, regenerative world if all humans felt love and kinship with the living beings of Earth? If humans created respectful, responsible, reciprocal, resonant relationships among our kin? These are ways of life, not isolated concepts, in most Indigenous and First Nations societies.

Here is my story of environmental activism in the hope that it will spark ideas for others. Over decades, my feelings of love for the Earth moved from "Nature worship" (for lack of a better term) to understanding and feeling myself within the interconnected Web of Life. My environmental activism ramped up following the first Vermont Witchcamp as if by magic. During a trance journey at the end of our work with the *Twelve Wild*

Swans, Starhawk asked, "What part of the wild will you stand for, will you speak for?" For me: the trees. As we say in sacred space, *What happens between the worlds changes all the worlds.* Within a month after camp, I received an unsolicited call from a city supervisor asking me to serve on the planning commission. As a commissioner, I drafted our tree protection ordinance. I also began writing an environmental column for a local paper.

Like many Reclaiming Witches, I've taken part in marches, rallies, meeting disruptions, and other forms of street activism. I've raised voice and pen against a local pipeline as well as against international fracked gas and oil infrastructure and for divestment of fossils. I've worked between the worlds with Starhawk, Laurie Lovekraft, and other pagans to create change via magical activism: scrubbing or burning away roots of injustice, fostering new growth of justice and liberation, working with nonhuman Allies. But the mainstay of my life's work: writing and teaching – the key forms my magical activism take.

A presenter at an environmental education conference spoke of crafting story to urge action and create change. He offered examples and theories to show how story (not facts and data) change beliefs. After that presentation, I delved into the cognitive science of narrative and story, a wonderful segue to the 2016 workshops I offered with Starhawk, "Stories for the Future." From our workshop description:

> Stories shape our imagination and our ideas of the possible. How can we use the power of story to help us envision a positive future, and inspire people to want to work towards it? Stir in a little magic – the art of shaping and shifting consciousness, of connecting with the deep creative energies of nature, bending time and opening awareness.

Participants were mostly pagan. I love to bring my work to mainstream audiences. For instance, I offered "Restorying a

Regenerative Future" at an international conference of the sustainability education center I co-founded at Columbia University. Another instance of magic in the mundane: after presenting the science of plant communication, I brought middle grade teachers outside to talk with trees using a method practiced among Reclaiming Witches. Then we discussed how to integrate such experiential exercises in their science curricula. Teaching and facilitating are forms that my magical activism takes.

Writing is another form my magical activism takes. While I've written nonfiction articles about nature, sustainability, and environmental activism, I prefer to read fiction. And as I mentioned, story is a powerful influencer. Thus, I write short- and long-form speculative fiction for wide audiences in service to a just, regenerative world.

My notions of activism continue to evolve, and I continue to write stories and novels. I welcome you to view my latest musings and info on my website: brightflame.com.

As a white settler on Turtle Island, it's important to acknowledge that the power and importance of story as well as living in right relationship within the Web of Life is not new to Indigenous and First Nations people. In my teaching and my nonfiction writing, I highlight the work of Indigenous scientists and educators such as Robin Wall Kimmerer of the Citizen Potawatomi Nation and Tewa educator Gregory Cajete (Santa Clara Pueblo), both distinguished university faculty and noted authors.

Memory: Earth Activism Exercise
Raven Edgewalker

Activism? Who among us consider ourselves activists? One of the three legs of the cauldron of Reclaiming is considered to be activism, and as we begin to explore the element of Earth we want to focus on environmental activism.

I was sitting in a circle, co-teaching Elements of Magic, the first of the Reclaiming core classes.

The previously noisy group became silent, eyes cast down, shoulders hunched, not wanting to look at anyone in case we picked a volunteer to start. The two of us leading the group got up and dragged our chairs to opposite ends of the rooms and climbed on them.

"Okay, **anyone who recycles everything possible**, walk down to this end of the space and stand there, anyone who recycles nothing, go walk down to the opposite end of the space and stand there."

Most of the group clustered around the centre of the space.

"Okay, what do you recycle? Share it with the person next to you."

The responses filled the haul: paper, glass, cardboard, metal, plastic, fabric and more...

Recycling is an act of environmental activism, recycling, even just using curbside recycling schemes keeps useful materials out of landfill sites.

I can see the group beginning to relax, heads coming up, shoulders relaxing as they begin to hope they're not about to be shamed by the lack of action, shamed by their own internal stories of what it means to be an environmental activist.

Who here is trying to reduce their plastic consumption? Maybe using cloth shopping bags or carrying reusable water bottles? Move towards one end if you do this most of the time, or the other end if you never do. This time, the whole group shuffles to the same end of the space – some clutching metal water bottles. We ask them to connect with each other – eye-to-eye or heart-to-heart, to see each other as allies.

Eight million metric tons of plastic end up in our oceans each year. While as an individual we can't make much of an impact, any impact helps.

Who, in this group, mends or repairs their clothes? Who buys clothes secondhand rather than new? People move about the room, most folk spread on either side of the centre. No one stands at the end of the room associated with "never". We encourage people to share ideas and stories with each other. We notice people proudly showing off patches, and items of clothing that are vintage or second-hand special finds.

Textile production is estimated to be responsible for about 20% of global clean water pollution. So called fast fashion has a huge environmental impact, contributes to the volume of waste filling landfill sites as well as frequently being produced in unsafe, poorly paid factories in Asia.

Next (people know the process now), **who uses public transport?** There's a big spread this time, from the always end of the room to the rarely/never end, but no one stands at either extreme.

We encourage folk to look at each other, to connect, to notice and not to judge. A few people feel uncomfortable and we invite them to fight the urge to justify and accept, inviting them to remember that this is just where they are in the present. Being uncomfortable is fine, it's good information and can provoke change.

Let's add in bikes and walking... People shift around, mostly between the centre and always parts of the space with fewer people towards the rarely/never end. The energy in the group shifts more.

Road transport accounts for 22% of total UK emissions of carbon dioxide (CO_2), one of the largest contributors to climate change globally.

Who has ever signed a petition or given money or time to an environmental cause – Greenpeace, Standing Rock for example? There's a stampede this time, everyone in the group has done something…from the conversations it's clear that many people frequently engage in this kind of activism.

Many seem to carry this story that we're only "proper" activists if we are on the streets marching, getting arrested or chained to trees and fences to prevent destruction of habitat. Some of us are able to do this, some of us aren't for a multiplicity of reasons. Some may be able to support those people who are doing this, some of us need to take on different roles and actions that are sustainable for us, for where we are now, in this moment. There are so many different ways of being an activist and so many ideas that we've not had time to consider in this workshop.

"Who in this group considers themselves, after all these ideas, to be an environmental activist?" This time the group all moves towards the end of the space that we've called "yes." We invite folk to connect with each other again in some way – through eye contact, through physical contact, through a few words or a story.

We call people back into the circle. We take a breath together and another, and we invite people to find in the silence of our breath one thing, one act, one action that they are willing to weave into their lives to take their activism further.

We invite them to drop their ideas and commitments into the space in the centre of our circle, some folk share a word, some an idea or a phrase, we begin to weave the words together into a cauldron of sound, the words become less distinct, people begin to move more, to dance, to touch, to hum and tone, the energy feels tangible, pulsing, and becomes wilder, as it begins to rise we raise our arms to the skies swaying together sending the energy up through the ceiling, and drinking it in to our bodies to support the work we've just taken on.

We look around the circle of people, eyes shining now and we all state "I am an activist."

Ritual & Magick

Ritual for Environmental Activism
Gaiamore

Ritual exists in many forms in the Reclaiming tradition. Coming together in a magical setting, we combine our inner work and spiritual work to strengthen our bond with others in a shared vision. The focused energy of the ritual carries our intention to the world, and the support of others sustains us as we go forth. Vermont Witchcamp ritual planners created this ritual in 2017 to honor and unite our various forms of activism against systems of oppression. The same outline can be transformed and embellished to suit any type of activism.

Ritual Intention

To recognize, honor and support the many types of environmental activism and envision the power we have together.

Note: This describes an outdoor ritual with a central fire. Where fire is not possible, any natural objects can be used for symbols of activism with the same effect of seeing them come together at the end for a powerful visual and emotional experience of power together.

Ritual Set-up

1. Create stations with signs indicating different forms of environmental activism (e.g. protest marches, electoral activism, working within the system, personal practices, supporting environmental organizations financially, by-any-means-necessary, community programs, etc.). The number of signs depends on how many participants (some can be combined). Supply string or yarn at each station.

2. Instruct participants to bring a stick to the ritual representing the way they contribute to caring for the Earth. Upon arriving at the ritual, participants place their stick at one of the stations that best describes their form of activism.

Gather, ground and invoke sacred space with the ritual intention in mind.

Body of Ritual

1. Go to your chosen station.
2. Discuss your form of activism with others while creating a simple sculpture with the sticks (and yarn).
3. Re-group at the central fire.
4. Groups present their sculptures and a spokesperson summarizes the group experience.
5. After each presentation, everyone responds with "We see you, we hear you, we thank you!!"

Raising Energy

Raise energy with a chant or tone as each group tosses their stick sculpture into the central fire. The flames rise up as a symbol of our power together as environmental activists, and the energy raised sends our intention out to the world. Open the circle with gratitude for all that was invoked.

Offerings
Marcos Bisticas-Cocoves

Baltimore, the city where I live, has three main watersheds. The Herring Run is one of them; it flows down the east side and into the Back River, itself an estuary connected to the Chesapeake Bay. Like many urban streams, the Herring Run does not get the love it deserves: its waters stink too often of sewage and its banks are littered with garbage. Blue Water Baltimore, our local watershed group, organized a stream cleaning a few years ago; some members of Baltimore Reclaiming's Activist Cell, myself included, showed up on a Saturday morning to help gather trash. Besides us, there were maybe thirty other volunteers: neighbors, families, and college students. For some, it was community service; for me, it was a form of magical activism, a spell of sorts. In particular, it was an *offering* to the stream and to the plants and animals who depend on it.

Understanding this simple work as a magical offering reframes it in useful ways. What is an offering, after all? In this case, at least, it is a *gift* from one concrete being to another. Concreteness is important here: I am making an offering to *this particular* stream or *this particular* stand of trees; another stream or other trees might have different needs. And the best gift takes the specific needs and desires of the recipient into consideration. For some plants, a water libation is the perfect offering; for others, it would cause harm. The Fae may love cream, but it might damage a tree. Reframing my environmental activism as a series of offerings allows me to center the specificity of each piece as an ecosystem.

It is possible, but not necessary, to integrate a kind of animism into this process. The conceptual and political advantage of animism in this and similar situations is to emphasize the uniqueness and integrity of a part of an ecosystem, be it a stream or a tree or a mountain. Animism need not be true, but it points to a truth: The concrete, non-human beings that make up our world are owed care and respect.

When most people think of a religious offering, though, they think of a positive gift: first fruits, a libation, a sacrifice. And many Witches, myself included, make similar positive offerings. I might go to my special place in the woods and offer a flower, a poem, or a breath.

Yet more and more, these offerings seem inadequate to me.

A beautiful wreath does not clean a polluted stream. Artfully-stacked stones might disrupt its flow. Nowadays, my standard offering is not to give something, but to take something away. Each day presents opportunities for offerings: For example, it's not difficult to find a plastic bag in the bushes beside any of the streams near my home. I slowly fill it with the detritus of people who love the stream and its banks in their own way: as a place for celebration, as a refuge from the noise of the city, sometimes even as a place to pitch a home. To remove these traces is not to erase humanity from the picture, but to transform our relation to the waters, in a way, is more caring and respectful.

These kinds of offerings, though necessary, are inadequate. The mounds of garbage we collected at the Herring Run go to a landfill. The stench of the sewer remains. Sometimes, the harm to individuals, human and non-human, cannot be made right. And, on a larger scale, species disappear, the tides rise, and the world boils. It seems impossible to repair the world, especially if repair means restoration to a previous state. We are caught between the impossibility and necessity of change.

What is the way out of this paradox? Perhaps we need more powerful magical tools for the more radical need that confronts us. What would it mean to conceive of larger social and political transformations in magical terms? What if a revolution is but a rite of passage for an entire society, an initiation, a death and rebirth, a metamorphosis?

A Queer, Biodiverse Blessing
Fighting the Wild and the Strange River Fagan

In 2003, I was a queer, non-binary college student in sleepy East Lansing, Michigan. I'd never been to Witchcamp, never taken any of the core Reclaiming classes, never even met a Reclaiming Witch. I had read Starhawk's books and blog posts, and also the Reclaiming Principles of Unity.

Isolated as I was, Reclaiming's vision was still bright enough to spark a passionate fire within me. Lit up with the knowledge that another world was possible, that activism and spirituality could be as intertwined as the systems of oppression we yearned to transform, I threw myself into the anti-war movement. As the Bush administration prepared to invade Iraq, I did almost everything I could think of to stop it. I went to countless meetings, protests, teach-ins, banner making parties, movie nights about the history of U.S. imperialism, potlucks, meetings about how other meetings had gone or would go or should go, and on and on.

But how, you might be wondering, was this environmental activism? We'll get there.

First, a bit more backstory. Through my flurry of anti-war organizing, I became close friends with, well, let's call him Sammy. Sammy was a few years younger than me, a trans guy estranged from his family and struggling intensely in a very queerphobic and hostile world. Like many young queers, his sense of worth had been deeply wounded by the message repeated by his family, by the churches, by the politicians, by the media – there's something wrong with you. And so, like many young queers, he wrestled with the impulse to kill himself.

This profound devaluing of queerness, of difference, of that which can't or won't fit into the neatly proscribed boxes demanded by oppressive, patriarchal order exactly mirrors the violent desecration of the wild, of wilderness, of all the life that wanders and spreads and can't be reduced to profitable "resources" by industrial capitalism. (And both of these mirror the demonization of the foreign, the "uncivilized," the "dangerous Other" that appears as an obstacle to the hungry expansion of Empire.)

From a Reclaiming perspective, from an eco-magical perspective, fighting to value and protect one's queer self, fighting to value and protect the wild, fighting to value and protect distant lands from imperial war—these are all facets of the same sacred impulse. The concept of biodiversity is relevant here. Just as a forest needs a variety of species to truly flourish, so does a human community need a range of gender expressions and sexual orientations to thrive. Just as the validity and rightness of an oak tree's lifeway does not detract from (and in fact supports) the very different lifeway of a squirrel or a mushroom or a fern, so too are many human lifeways right and beautiful and necessary.

Back to Sammy. Sammy and I bonded through our shared queerness, our similar dark, edgy senses of humor, and our shared interest in witchy spiritual practices. For both of us, in fighting to stop the war, we were also fighting for a world free of patriarchal, industrial, and imperial control. A world in which both our queerness and the wilderness were seen as the sacred, worthy things they were, and therefore respected and allowed to flourish.

Sammy confided in me his fantasies of taking his own life in a way that would serve this cause – of a political suicide that would somehow stop the gears of the machine grinding mercilessly towards invasion. And so when he came up with a plan to chain himself to a car as part of a protest blockade of a gas station, I was conflicted. I wasn't sure if this was a drastic but proportional response to a dire situation or a form of self-harm. I wasn't sure if my close friend was fighting to value and protect himself and the wild or if he was throwing his own value away. I wanted to support him and honor his choice and also, I was scared about his well-being.

And so I called up my witch's wisdom and power and did what I could do.

With Sammy's consent, I wrote an elemental blessing for him and spoke the words in sacred space, blessing and empowering him and his action. I wish I had saved or remembered the blessing but I no longer have it with me. I remember the gist though. I called upon the elements of life–Air, Fire, Water, Earth, and Mystery–to watch over and protect my friend, to amplify the power of his brave protest, to spread his message of how wrong and unnecessary the war was, weaving with the broader spell chanted and spoken and stamped across countless signs: NO BLOOD FOR OIL.

In that blessing, I was a punk rock priestess. I was a lonely, self-taught, Midwestern queer kid who'd learned magic from books using the power of that lineage, that stream of words to bless another queer misfit. I was a Reclaiming witch casting a spell to support my friend in aligning his complex action with his deepest intention: to value and protect the wild, the strange, within and beyond himself.

Now, almost twenty years later, the magic of that spell is still needed. My friend, thank the Goddex, is alive and well, tending his own queer, chosen, multi-generational family. Less happily, imperialism and queerphobia and the relentless destruction of the wild are also still alive and well.

My dream and prayer and spell for Reclaiming is that we truly deepen into and embody and live out our beautiful values. May we become a tradition that is even more biodiverse, a tradition that reaches far beyond liberal coastal enclaves in the U.S. to inspire and empower lonely queer kids in forgotten cities in the Midwest as well as activists and outcasts all over the world, a tradition that transforms and is transformed by people of color, trans and non-binary people, working class and poor people, and all the most marginalized, a tradition that centers nourishing justice, fierce liberation, and wild love.

Magical Media Workings to Protect The Forests
Celia 'Sorrel' Alario

I was a DIY pagan first, an environmental activist next, and eventually, a part of the Reclaiming Family. But well before I'd ever been to a Spiral Dance this community had my back, and Reclaiming witches were magically protecting me and supporting my media work to amplify environmental activism.

It was 1996 and I was engaged with North Coast Earth First! (EF!) and Rainforest Action Network on behalf of the Headwaters Redwood Forests of Humboldt County. Reclaiming was a spiritual backbone of the frontline forest defense movement that season, conjuring justice with their own distinct flavor of Divinity. Their presence was palpable, their rituals buoying.

My travel and placement onto the EF! Media team was coordinated in part by a spirited and magical woman, who I'd come to recognize later as a powerful priestess and Reclaiming community member. She shared a list of supplies needed and invited me to join her in a multiplier spell, a forest activist style loaves and fishes maneuver by which sufficient donations would be manifested to meet the ever-growing needs of a basecamp full of folks committed to creative confrontation and nonviolent direct action to protect the forest.

I stopped in the Bay Area to hit up climbing and outdoor equipment stores for donations, and literally filled my car to the brim with food and gear donations. My first Reclaiming-supported spell had worked, and as I placed the last box of Clif Bars into the car, I contemplated the drive to the Redwoods without the use of my rearview mirrors, trusting that the forces that filled the car would guide my way.

My big brother Jack suggested that, since I was going to help out with the media work, Mercury and Hermes and Hanuman would be good allies along the journey, so we found room to squeeze that trifecta of tricksters into my VW Golf as well.

The Reclaiming activists taught me we could put multiplier spells on our media calls too, ritualizing the publicity work and press calls (we were FAXING press releases by hand back then) and I began a practice of blending prayer and ritual with 'work' which I continue to this day. This act of making the mundane sacred extended into my years of communications and media work for Mama Earth.

The focal point for action at Headwaters was Fisher Gate, where every morning before the logging trucks arrived activists would create a blockade. I was on a 'need to know basis' as the media person, which meant that I'd be awakened each morning (at my sleeping spot under the computer desk) and given details of who was at Fisher Gate, how they'd designed this particular blockade and get the quotes I'd need to begin my morning ritual at the fax machine.

I'll always remember the Samhain ritual that year, where the Reclaiming team painted faces and carved pumpkins infusing them with spells designed to be released when the pumpkins were smashed. Their pumpkins were spread out across the road at Fisher Gate, forming a 'soft blockade', nothing that would block access for long. But as the loggers in their massive trucks ran the pumpkins over (sometimes backing up and smashing them repeatedly to taunt us) they were perplexed to hear the witches cheer. That was a story that didn't need to be pitched to reporters, those spells would do their work without a media spotlight. And one of those sacred squash was infused with a prayer for me and others out front of the media team, that we stay safe and that all obstacles be removed in our efforts to garner national attention that could catalyze a deal to save the ancient forests. Those spells worked.

A few years later, I was on the streets of Seattle, doing media for groups taking on the Earth destroying forces of the World Trade Organization. For days I was in the flow, and myriad synchronicities helped me steward journalists into all the right places at the right times. I'd noticed two beautiful sparkly women who always seemed to be where I was. I finally approached them only to find that they were Reclaiming witches who'd committed to shadow me on the streets, to protect me and work media magic alongside my publicity efforts.

Suddenly the extent of my success made much more sense. I felt so blessed to be supported and protected by these Reclaiming members, part of my own magical media team amplifying my momentum.

Every media team working for a just and livable future deserves its own team of Reclaiming protectorates. May we find a way to shadow more of our eco-media makers, and extend our cone of protection over clipboards, cell phones, emails and bullhorns on front lines everywhere! So mote it be!

An Extinction Rebellion Ritual
Sylvia Rose

First, we gather to share our ideas and information about XR. Some of us are committed activists, some have been arrested during rebel acts and give first-hand accounts. Some are too disabled for street actions and have supported the rebellion in other ways. Some have never heard of XR and wonder whether it even exists in their own country.

To begin the ritual we create sacred space. We cast a circle to surround ourselves with a protective working bubble. We invoke the elements of air, fire, water and earth, the powers of above, below and centre.

In love and rage, together and separately, we call our demands. We address those both greater and smaller, the universal and the individual. We call each XR demand in turn, repeating it again and again, a low murmur, as others voice their own details, building a bigger picture.

"Act now, act now, act now..."
"I call on all world leaders, corporations, and businesses to act before it's too late"
"Act today"
"I call on my local council to become carbon neutral by 2025"
"Listen to the scientists and act on their advice"
"Decarbonisation now!"
"Social justice now"

"Tell the truth, tell the truth, tell the truth..."
"Tell the truth in our schools and to our children!"
"Be honest about the dangers that face us"
"Newspapers and media, take climate change seriously"
"Beyond politics, beyond politics, beyond politics..."
"Create citizens' assemblies and act on their recommendations"
"Act beyond political parties. I call on all politicians to come together to face this crisis"
"Listen to the people"
"We demand participatory democracy"

As the calls subside, in silence we each draw our own XR symbol on a circle of wood, as a token and talisman, thinking what we might ourselves do once we return home to support the work of XR and other climate change movements worldwide. No pressure, no obligations, just commitments to ourselves and maybe to our Godds. Some draw an image on the obverse of their disc, to remind themselves later of their visioning. Holding our symbols, one by one as the spirit moves us, we name our pledges.

"I will attend at least one local meeting."
"I will talk to others, let more people know about XR."
"If there is no group where I live, I will set one up."

As each one speaks, the group affirms their pledge.

"We hear you."

We feel the power of being witnessed and supported, the power of community.

And finally we raise energy to support our work, to support the work of Extinction Rebellion and related movements, to charge the very symbol itself with power. We sing:

"We are the tongue that speaks the truth
We are the song on the wind
We are the courage to step forth
We are the change that now begins."

We raise and combine our voices to a wordless cone of power, with all our love and hope and passion and rage. The cone coheres and spirals and rises, and then falls gently back to the earth, to rest and spread and empower.

In closing, we say our thanks and farewells to the elements. We open our circle and go our separate ways, our hearts charged with love and determination. And hope that one by one, ritual by ritual, action by action, country by country, our voices will be heard and we can bring about the urgent changes we all need.

Looking Ahead

To Be Real
David Samas

People make me sick;
and wilderness is the treatment.

The mountain spirit swells toward the sky
breathing the immortal life force of light
and exhaling deep and ancient forests
full of deer and songbirds.

People make me sick;
and wilderness is the treatment.

It is not enough to eat the venison and imagine the air
and pretend to be a part of nature
while all the time obsessing over saving 1.99 on cans of tuna.

To be real:

Walk barefoot everyday for half an hour,
breathe deeply with a living tree,
stare into the brilliant sun at dawn,
and share one body with the kingdom of plants
who's spirits and selfless giving made this world inhabitable;
share your water with the streams,
and sit by the fire,
singing to the stars from which we've come;

burning in the bleak
darkness
to which we all shall go.

The Sacred Earth, Our Only Home
Cassidy Brown

There is a place I like to go alone. Just me and my pack, heavy with food and shelter for a night or two. Near a river bank, far enough from the trail you'd have to be looking to see it, is a small fire ring with several massive cedars standing around it, their lowest branches too high to catch the flying sparks. I go there to be with the mountain, the river, and most of all, the trees.

The first time I discovered the place I had just received my Reiki II attunement and I knew my life had changed in some way. Standing on the bank among the cedars I felt settled and strong, with my power ready within me for whatever direction I chose. Which direction, though, was still uncertain. I climbed a 5-foot-tall fallen cedar trunk and placed my hands gently on the even larger tree standing beside it. Stilling my mind, I decided to try offering reiki to the cedar. I waited for a yes or a no, my palms beginning to tingle with the healing energy.

What I got from the tree surprised me. Something along the lines of, "What could you have that I need?" I could feel its energy running powerfully up and down, coursing like a mighty river. And here I was with my half-cup of water trying to help it out! I laughed. What, indeed, could a mostly-domesticated, well-meaning, but directionless human hope to offer to a being older than my great-grandparents? I asked the question: "Is there any wisdom you can offer me?" After a while I seemed to feel an answer.

Don't be one who kills and takes away. I saw a vision of a hunting bobcat, killing for its meal but remaining within the ecosystem so the life it takes is returned to the forest. Then an image of the clear cuts on the other side of the hill – the logs and their precious carbon carted off to build suburbs in Asia, far away from the soil that fed them and the creatures that rely on their shelter for survival.

Be a home to others. Stay and feed your children when you die.

I looked at the log I was sitting on and saw the ferns, mosses, insects, shrubs, and even a couple ten-inch cedar saplings growing out of its slowly decaying body. Looking up at the live tree above me, I saw more mosses, lichens, birds, insects, and squirrels, just in the lower branches. *Be a home...*

Years later in a drab hotel room in the desert I read an article that opened my eyes to the reality of the climate crisis – the droughts, the floods, the fires, the waters rising, the species lost forever (three every hour, every day)[1] due to our greed, our blindness, our endless "killing and taking away." It hit me hard. As if every twenty minutes I lost a dear friend – an extinct fish, plant, insect, or mammal, each a key to its ecosystem's wellness. I wept. Grief settled in my stomach like 88 pounds of plastic in the belly of a whale dying of starvation.[2] Grief dissolved into the fluids of my body like the million tons of industrial waste dumped into the streams of my home state.[3] Rage at these atrocities tore through my heart like the ten million acres that burned in wildfires last year.[4] It was too much. How could I hope to metabolize the rage and grief of an entire planet in my human body?

I got sick. I got very sick. The illness had biological causes, but I felt this world-sized grief was part of why my body had suddenly decided to shut down. My doctor asked me if I had experienced any stress or trauma recently. I tried to explain my awakening to the climate emergency. "Anything closer to home, though?" she asked. Closer to home than the actual planet we live on that provides for our existence? "No," I answered.

Another doctor listened more closely. "Do you think you are an empath?" she asked, "or maybe, and this might sound weird, but an empath for the planet or nature?"

Not weird at all to a witch, I thought. "Aren't we all?" I said, "We are a part of the Earth. Its trauma is our trauma. There is no real separation, people just forget." I realized that is the root of my practice and my spirituality: not forgetting. This is the work of

Reclaiming Witches in particular – with our roots in ecofeminist politics and our branches reaching toward ecstatic visions – to help others remember the sacredness and interconnectedness of the Earth and ourselves.

> *To consider something sacred is to say that it is profoundly important, that it has a value in and of itself that goes beyond our immediate comfort and convenience, that we don't want to see it diminished or denigrated in any way. The word "sacred" comes from the same root as "sacrifice" ... If something is sacred to us, we are willing to sacrifice something to protect it, willing to take a stand or to risk ourselves in its service.* – Starhawk[5]

In Reclaiming there is a chant we sing that goes: *Earth my body, water my blood, air my breath, and fire my spirit!* It reminds me that I am woven from the powerful forces of nature, the same ones that make up the cedars, the river, and the mountain. And it reminds me that these elements of my being are merely on loan. Someday I will return them. I hope when they are released and unraveled from myself they will "stay and feed the children," human and sapling. I don't have an answer for the climate crisis, or for my chronic illness. There is no quick fix, only trying things to see if they help, choosing one less-bad option after another, praying, and learning. When I feel into the Earth, I sense her energy coursing strong like the cedar's. In spite of everything her magic is alive, and so is mine. To honor them I try to "be a home to others" in my community, and to give back to our shared home – the living Earth, source of all that is sacred.

Notes

1. Doyle, Alister. "U.N. Urges World to Slow Extinctions: 3 Each Hour," May 22, 2007. *reuters.com,* https://www.reuters. com/article/us-climate-extinctions/u-n-urges-world-to-slow-extinctions-3-each-hour-idUSL2253331920070522

2. Mortada, Dalia. "Stomach of Dead Whale Contained 'Nothing But Nonstop Plastic,'" March 18, 2019. *npr.org*, https://www.npr.org/2019/03/18/704471596/stomach-of-dead-whale-contained-nothing-but-plastic

3. "1,290,750 Pounds of Toxic Chemicals Dumped into Oregon's Waterways," June 19, 2014. *environmentoregon.org*, https://environmentoregon.org/news/ore/1290750-pounds-toxic-chemicals-dumped-oregon's-waterways

4. "Facts + Statistics: Wildfires," April 8, 2021. *iii.org*, https://www.iii.org/fact-statistic/facts-statistics-wildfires

5. Starhawk. *The Earth Path: Grounding Your Spirit in the Rhythms of Nature.* HarperCollins, 2004.

This Activism Stuff is Not for Me. And Yet.
Fortuna Sawahata

It's January 2007, and I'm standing in the parking lot of a former low-security detention facility in Cazadero, in the hills of West Sonoma.

It's the *activist* part of the Earth Activist Training (EAT) and some of my co-students and the program administrators are showing how to lock arms – literally – to create a human barrier, an important technique in public activism. The rest of us are meant to run forward, rushing the human wall, to test its effectiveness.

My stomach drops awkwardly. It kind of rattles, sinking from side to side, like a metal box with a brick inside. This is nothing more than a practical demonstration; still, I feel like I'm going to poop myself. I'm embarrassed by my apparent immobilisation in the face of (theoretical) violence. I watch the clued-up, already-active activists mixing it up. They know the rules. It's an exhibition game for them.

To try to save face I do what I remember doing during sporty games in grammar school: lurk on the edges, pretending I'm helping the team. At least not hindering them. It's a pretty weak stance. Pretty weak. Like the excuses my Talker keeps coming up with, arguments on behalf of my frightened Fetch: I'm turning 50 this year, and this kind of activism is really a young person's game. Or, I've got a stellium in Libra in the first house – I'm a lover, not a fighter, etc. etc.

And yet

I'm here for my foundational Design Certificate in Permaculture. I want to do it with Starhawk, in a magical way. The fact of my being here is an inexplicable leap of my own wild heart – a piece of personal activism, and of magic: I've wanted to do the EAT since I first read about it, but had no idea at all how I would pay, take time off of work, etc. Stars, money and time have aligned to fulfil this desire. While my partner must think this is just an expensive whim, he'll be happy to have the house and cat to himself for a few weeks.

A chain of synchronicities

There's more to this EAT, this desire to learn more about magickal environmental activism: I'm a novice to the tradition, but Reclaiming is apparently on the cards for me. Baruch – one of the teaching team from my first Reclaiming Witchcamp in Belgium six months earlier – was calmly rolling a cigarette in the big mess of the Black Mountain Retreat Center in January 2007 when I arrived. It proves to be more than a nice surprise. The chain of synchronicities begins: next year, at my second Loreley Witchcamp in Belgium, I'll be Baruch's student teacher. The incredibly rewarding and absolutely surprising pathway to becoming a teacher at Reclaiming Witchcamps and workshops begins right here, right now.

But I have no idea about that as I throw myself (not literally) into the learnings of EAT.

Am I the worst activist in the world?

While I'm okay at singing 'The Bacteria Song', practically

speaking I'm a disaster. No one who sees my difficulty in determining where to dig a swale, my inability to swing a sledge hammer ('Use the weight of the tool!' snorts Stan W. impatiently), and my squeamishness about dry loos (although it was pretty amazing pooping into an empty Hebrew National Hot Dog bucket at Starhawk's cabin) can imagine me doing the rough-and-ready, hands-on work of being a permaculturist. And certainly not that of an activist.

But guess what?

I discover that the 12 Principles of Design that are the foundation of permaculture are also an exquisitely articulated guide to an activist's (witch's, parent's, artist's, banker's, etc.) life:

- Principle 1: Observe and interact
- Principle 2: Catch and store energy
- Principle 3: Obtain a yield
- Principle 4: Apply self-regulation and accept feedback
- Principle 5: Use and value renewable resources & services
- Principle 6: Produce no waste
- Principle 7: Design from patterns to details
- Principle 8: Integrate rather than segregate
- Principle 9: Use small and slow solutions
- Principle 10: Use and value diversity
- Principle 11: Use edges and value the marginal
- Principle 12: Creatively use and respond to change

From https://permacultureprinciples.com/principles/

Of these principles, one has become a quiet form of activism stuck in my psyche: the validation of Permaculture Principle 11: Use edges and value the marginal. For me this is one of the strengths of Reclaiming in general. The tradition actively engages in discussions arising from the edges of All the Worlds.

In the past 15 years of my being a member of Reclaiming, there is a visible trajectory of evolution, notably in the Principles of Unity. The edges and the marginal become part of the integrated whole, and in society as in permaculture this creates vitality.

Honouring the wild

"Wherever you go, there you are..."

"I would know myself in all my parts."

"The Peacock has ugly feet."

To honour the wild, I have to honour myself and my desires. Despite the dark and imperfect things. Radical self-love, that great cliché, is essential. We must love ourselves in our own essential wildness and imperfection, and trust that the chaos of desire – that spark and leap of absolute unflag-able interest/whim/attraction – is leading somewhere. (It doesn't always, mind you. But my Black Hearted whim – to do the EAT – led me to a huge part of who I am, which is a teacher.)

How do I practice activism? In the ways that I can, as an urban witch in a very crowded and noisy city. I plant wild plants that bees and insects love. I separate my trash, recycle, and buy local whenever possible. I pick up the zillion Red Bull cans scattered in the local park. As a witch I am aware of the lively consciousnesses of the trees and water around me, including the very urban little split of the River Rotte that runs right past my apartment building, supporting carp and swans.

Kindness and gratitude are a sort of activism too. It's so much easier to be fierce, fiery – well, active! Kindness, gratitude, and especially forgiveness of self and others are amongst the greatest tools of wholeness. These active practices are fundamental to a healthy life.

And so I want to honour just a tiny few of those who have brought me here, because if I list everyone it will be pages. To Starhawk, Baruch, David Holmgren, Thorn, Raven, Crow, and, of course, Irisanya, thank you.

The Next Generation: Nurturing Environmentalism in Reclaiming Kids
Laurie Lovekraft

The adrenaline rush during a direct action can't be compared. It's thrilling to risk arrest and use your chutzpah, skill, and magic in defense of mother earth. I've been involved with many environmental campaigns through the years and have experienced some powerful events: a cone of power propelling an activist off their feet and into a redwood tree, the tragic destruction of the South Central Farm, the saving of a 400-year-old oak named Old Glory, the mass arrest of 1,000 people, working at the historic Paris climate agreement, and a shareholder meeting for Occidental Petroleum where I addressed the villainous CEO / Chairman, Ray Irani.

Raising my children in the Reclaiming Tradition, I've looked for ways to involve them in my activism and foster their connection to the earth. After decades in the magical community, I know that just because someone wears a pentagram, celebrates the Wheel of the Year, or has an impressive crystal collection, doesn't mean they will join a climate justice rally. Or bring a reusable mug to a ritual. Or take action to protect, defend, and heal the earth.

It's false to assume that young people raised with earth-based spirituality will automatically become environmentalists. So, how do we create a natural, empathetic response towards the earth that will preempt apathy? How can ecological activism be seen as a joyful, empowering necessity, rather than an inconvenience?

Let It Begin

- Leading by example is one of the simplest approaches to take. Put down the screen, turn off the lights after leaving a room, turn off the faucet, and make these teachable moments for your kids. Start to speak honestly to them about the impact of climate change on frontline communities around the world and point out the roots of environmental racism in your home country.

- Honor your local bioregion and discover the native species and geology. Talk to kids about the First People of your area and its colonial history of oppression. Let children know that indigenous people get to speak for themselves and tell their own creation stories. Then read those stories together.

- Look for Patterns. "As above, so below, as within, so without" is a Hermetic phrase from the Emerald Tablet attributed to Hermes Trismegistus. It's microcosms and macrocosms. From the spiral of a seashell to the spiral on our fingertips and ears, to the spiral of a hurricane and galaxy. The five-petalled flower, a child's five-fingered hand, a five-legged sea star. This is the Principle of Correspondence, it recognizes small and large patterns – we are not separate from nature, we are part of it.

- Point out that the earth is alive. It is not a machine or the sum of its parts. It is a complex, living, open system. It is interdependent and interconnected, self-organized and self-stabilizing. Call it the Gaia Hypothesis if you have skeptical teens or explain to a younger child the wondrous flocking of birds in the sky.

- Talk about animism. Everything has a consciousness. Ask open-ended questions: what might a modern animistic worldview look like?

- Resist nature deficit disorder by getting out and experiencing the outdoors. Walk, drive, or take public transit to green spaces. Volunteer at tree plantings, tree care events, beach and river cleanups, and state park trail maintenance. Find an accessible park, public garden, or even a cemetery and spend time sitting, walking, skating, or rolling. Explore a neighborhood with mature trees – how different it feels from neighborhoods that are barren and hardscaped. Try geocaching if your kids insist on a technology tether.

- Reclaiming's annual summer camps – both Witchlets in the Woods and Redwood Magic Family Camp – have been essential for developing my children's ecological selves. Getting beyond cell phone range means they must entertain themselves, whether building forts in a massive redwood stump or playing Dungeons & Dragons at a sunny picnic table.

- We also need to teach young people as they grow older to think critically about the causes of the environmental crisis. Where the pressure points are in the system to disrupt how people think and behave, from shoppers to corporate executives to politicians:

"The locations of these types of interventions have included: the **point of production** where goods are produced (such as a factory or laboratory), the **point of destruction** where resources are extracted or pollution is dumped (such as a logging road or toxic waste site), the **point of consumption** where products are purchased (such as a chain store or a lunch counter) and the **point of decision** where the power-holders are located (such as a corporate headquarters or a congressional office)." (Re-Imagining Change, Doyle Canning & Patrick Reinsborough, 2009, page 27).

Talk to kids about the **point of assumption**, when – and where – do we learn that nature is a limitless commodity whose only value is usefulness to humans / capitalism, versus nature having its own inherent value.

How Will We Know?
When our children demand that we do more to protect, defend, and heal the earth, that's when we know our efforts are working.

When they lecture us about big oil subsidies, decommissioning dams, indigenous peoples' land rights, and building vibrant communities. When they ask to go for a hike. When they combine magic and activism, ritual and climate justice, that's when we will know. Especially, when we see a willingness to, "work in diverse ways, including nonviolent direct action, for all forms of justice: environmental, social, political, racial, gender and economic" (Reclaiming Principles of Unity).

Helpful Resources

- Reclaiming Family and Teen Camps (North America) Redwood Magic, Witchlets in the Woods, Teen Earth Magic
- "Teen Earth Magic! An Empowerment Workbook" by Luke Hauser
- "Campfire Chants: Songs for the Earth," by Reclaiming
- "Thinking Like a Mountain: Toward a Council of All Beings" by John Seed and Joanna Macy
- "Beautiful Trouble, a Toolbook for Revolution" by Andrew Boyd
- "The Yes Men Fix the World" directed by Andy Bichlbaum and Mike Bonanno, with Kurt Engfehr

Let Water Flow – how Reclaiming Magic Sustains my activism
SusanneRae

Written 2021 on the land of the Wilyakali people – who are part of the Barkindji Nation. I give my respects to the traditional custodians of the lands and to the elders, past, present and future. I acknowledge the harms caused by ongoing colonisation and acknowledge all those who keep culture and country strong into the deep future. By making this acknowledgment I commit to active and meaningful justice in my everyday life.

I stand on the edge of the road, before me stretching out to the horizon is a mighty lake. The sun reflected on the water causes me to raise my hand to shield my eyes. I turn to the west- water, to the east -water, behind me the mighty endless desert. The skeletons of giant trees reach to the sky. This is an ancient lake part of an extensive ephemeral system in the arid region of far western so-called NSW. For millennia this system has filled and drained with the rains. Rains that fall far to the north in tropical so-called Queensland and flow over months down the great Baaka river, spreading out across the flood plains and nourishing this great arid land. I stand on the edge of Menindee lake in Barkindji country, so called, NSW, Australia. The Baaka may be hard to find on a map because when the Europeans arrived in 1829, they renamed it the Darling River.

The Baaka is one part of the great river system known as the Murray-Darling Basin. This river system is the heart of so-called eastern Australia. A river basin second only in size to the Amazon. It stretches from the tropical north, the mountains in the east and empties into the Southern Ocean at the Coorong, in so-called South Australia. A complex system of creeks and rivers, billabongs, wetlands and lakes that has been home to so many nations pre-European invasion. A massive river system that brings life to forests, fields and towns across the eastern part of this continent.

Along the banks of the rivers the mighty red gums grow – so huge it takes fifteen to twenty paces to circle them. They hold the banks and their roots moving through the soil provide home for creatures to live and breed. In the lakes the fingerlings of the Murray River cod, eels, crayfish and turtles are born and grow.

I was born on the banks of this system, way to the northeast of Gamilaraay/Kamilaroi country, it is the first water I have known. Over the six decades of my life I have travelled and met its many rivers and waters, developing a deep love relationship with this system. I have also witnessed its demise.

Two months ago I stood here and there was no water. I camped beside the empty lake and watched the stars shift across the sky overnight. I was filled with grief. There had been rain up north, much rain in fact but it was dammed and held back. Two stolen floods, the locals say. But now the authorities have released some of the water they had been holding upstream. The water is pounding into the lake – it's so noisy, the weir open, the turbulence disconcerting. Industrial noise pollution in a natural environment. I can barely think.

I drive to the far side of the lake, about 20 kilometers and sit beside the water. It's flowing, yes, but it is quiet, too quiet. Apart from a few crows there is no life. The lake is lifeless. I weep a little. There has been no water in the lake for four years. Water blocked from flowing here – no water no life. No fish, crayfish, eels or water weed. In some parts of the lake the birds are returning –where the water is held for boating enthusiasts – far from here.

The region has seen one of the worst droughts in European history and in 2019 the largest fish kill in living memory. It is said millions of Murray River Cod, some one hundred years old, died that summer, when an algae bloom took the oxygen from the water. These fish had seen many droughts but because the water level was so low, they could not take refuge in the deeper water – it was gone.

The Australian and state governments privatised water on this land in the 1990's. Since then water rights have been bought and sold on the open market. The great Murray-Darling system has been entirely managed. Water held up north for cotton farmers and mines. Dams, weirs, pipelines and controlled flows have stressed the system to the point of breaking.

In 2002, I stepped over the Baaka at Wilcannia, this waterway where paddle steamers once travelled, was a single step wide. No words can describe the feeling I had that day.

The damming of the flows of water in so-called eastern

Australia is an act of continuing colonisation. Although native title was granted to the Barkindji in 2015 the water only flows from up north when the dams there are full. The Barkindji people are still losing their country.

This is what the water wars look like. It's happening here in 2021 in the "outback," a twelve-hour drive from so-called Sydney, where populations are sparse and the powerful think nobody is watching. In the papers, on social media and through the human airwaves there is much noise about irrigation, floodplain harvesting and environmental flows. About cotton, mining, water diversion and evaporation. Underneath is a rising voice, a strengthening calling out, asking who owns the water? Why is water being bought and sold? What share market portfolios deal in water? How can this be? And climate change...

Alone on the lake edge I watch the flow of water around the skeletal trunks of trees, the way the light flickers and feel the breeze on my face. The elements fire, air, earth, water and spirit are all here. I sit and breathe. There is beautiful deep sadness in the land and in me. A muscle shell, as big as my hand, lies halfway between where the water is and the shore line once was, about 20 meters behind me. I wonder if the lake will be allowed to fill that high again. I wonder if the water will stay long enough for life to return. Last time the lake was filled it was emptied to support downstream flows – I have been told, despite not being needed. And now they have already started to empty the lakes.

I watch the clouds reflected on the water and hear the crow call. The sun is warm on this cool autumn day. I offer the water a blessing, I tell the lake I am watching. I pledge to do my best and remember this article.

My initial contacts with Reclaiming style magic and activism occurred through the Women's Liberation Movement in the 1980's. Despite not being involved in a community for the next 30 years, my perceived understanding of earth-based magical activism prevailed and continued to shape me. It was there when I stepped over the river, it is there now as I sit by this troubled lake.

I am learning to listen to land – to read the seasons, hear its history, ancient and colonised. Open myself to communication with the original people of this place. To stand in a connected space and not to be overwhelmed by destruction, by the chaos. To look the mess that humanity has created directly in the eye.

Reclaiming magic holds me. It has offered tools of grounding, connecting and sustaining self in the here and now, whilst reaching into the recent and distant pasts, across time and multidimensional space. It offers me ways to connect to spirit and what is not seen. It is anchored in love of land and life. It aims to understand change and transformation. It is prepared to look at power and how it operates within, amongst and on us. I find the Principles of Unity a powerful supportive framework guide from which to work.

Knowing there are at least 500 people across the planet who have my back when I enter into political action, alone or with my reclaiming community is profoundly empowering. Their support strengthens me even if we don't know each other's name.

In a Reclaiming camp ritual I married the earth. I learned my purpose could be to speak for the land in places it cannot. Since then I have used my voice to speak for trees in local council meetings, wildlife in local papers, written articles and blog posts, walked with red-rebels to draw attention to climate change, sung to the land and spoken to strangers about the river. I have participated in demonstrations and calls to action, sometimes huge and sometimes small local acts. Sometimes alone or with one other. Most recently I sewed a banner with magical intent that was tied to a boat, part of flotillas demanding flows in the river system.

The work I do in camp and community sustains and nurtures me. I am challenged and held at the same time. Through reclaiming there is an opportunity to interrogate my conditioning and wounds so that when I step out, speak up I am less afraid or intimidated. There is a system of understanding and relationship, based in the natural world that I relate to. And it works with me.

Reclaiming has helped me to understand and take responsibility for my privilege using it to heal, to make reparations; to support my change and growth as a witch and as a human on this planet with responsibility for what is wild.

Conclusion

"A real relationship with nature is vital for our magical and spiritual development, and our psychic and spiritual health. It is also a vital base for any work we do to heal the earth and transform the social and political systems that are assaulting her daily." Starhawk, *The Earth Path*

I personally find that telling me what to do is not the way to get me to do something. But if you inspire me with story and personal connection, you have my attention. My hope with this compilation is not just to give you a peek into Reclaiming Witchcraft and its activism (albeit an incomplete narrative), but also to offer you a whisper of some of the voices who were there. Where it happened. Where it still happens.

I am an aggressively hopeful person. Someone who does believe in change and possibility. I believe in potential and creative approaches that come out of necessity. Out of being in the time that we're in. While it is true that this world can look so bleak and there may be no turning back from ecological damage, I personally don't believe all is lost. Call me naive. Call me whatever you like.

I honor the wild. And all of the ways the wild inspires, surprises, and holds. Whatever comes next is going to look different. Whatever is on the horizon is going to take all of our wisdom and wonder, all of our hope and desire. No doubt. And I think the Earth is worth it.

Contributors

Celia 'Sorrel' Alario has spent more than three decades helping environmental justice activists and human rights thought leaders hone their voices and build a better future. Known to some as the 'Priestess of Pleasure,' she cultivates joy and sacredness in the mundane from the red rock deserts to the sea.

Marcos Bisticas-Cocoves (he/him) is a philosopher and member of Baltimore Reclaiming.

Randy Blaustein is cis Queer Femme of Ashkenazi Jewish descent, who is an Anderson Feri initiate & also circles with Reclaiming. Her first model for social justice & environmental activism was her Mom, Alice; this piece is dedicated to Alice's memory.

BrightFlame (she/they) writes, teaches and makes magic in service to a just, regenerative future. She lives with her partner in Lenape territory (Eastern U.S.) among sassafras, oak, hickory and other wild ones. www.brightflame.com

Cassidy Brown (any pronoun) is a queer witch and priestess who was born and raised among the mighty trees along the Willamette River in Oregon. They are passionate about bringing earth-based, immanent spirituality to people in prisons and the community by writing, teaching, and leading embodied, ecstatic ritual.

Kim Chilvers (she/her) is a therapist, witch and activist who can often be seen hugging trees.

Georgie Craig (she/her) is a witch and Reclaiming teacher who lives in San Rafael, CA.

Raven Edgewalker (they/them) is a British Witch, Teacher and Priest in the Reclaiming and Anderson Feri Traditions. They are an inveterate upcycler of random and unconsidered trifles and collector of sticks. www.worldtreelyceum.org

River Fagan (they/them) is a therapist, writer, and witch living in Portland, OR. You can find out more at riverfagan.com

George Franklin (aka Luke Hauser) teaches magic and writes fiction, nonfiction, and lots of emails. Find his books (print or free downloads) at http://directaction.org/freebies

Gaiamore (Gail Morrison) is a teacher, artist, and eco-therapist who created a tool for Nature Divination called The Earth Deck. She has been a Reclaiming Teacher since 1995.

Laurie Lovekraft (she/her) is a priestess, performer, and writer who co-founded Reclaiming Los Angeles and Redwood Magic Family Camp. She is raising her children in the Reclaiming Tradition and makes her home in the Ballona Creek Watershed, Southern California Coast Bioregion (Gabrielino/Tongva peoples' traditional, ancestral, and unceded territory).

Irisanya Moon (she/they) is a Moon Books author, teacher/facilitator, poet, and initiate in the Reclaiming Witchcraft tradition. Her magick focuses on matters of the heart and their ongoing work with life as a love spell. www.irisanyamoon.com

Shannon Rose Raison (she/her) is a queer settler of Polish, Irish, English, and German descent living on Quw'utsun territories where she dreams, writes, and works as a sex worker and counsellor. She has been a Reclaiming witch since 2015 when a dream brought her down the coast of Turtle Island to her first California Witchcamp.

Sylvia Rose has been a witch in the Reclaiming tradition for many years. She lives in the UK and has helped organise many of the witchcamps there, both Avalon and then Dragonrise. She also lives with ME/Chronic Fatigue Syndrome.

David Samas is a queer/two spirit, SF native polymath composer, cosmologist, conceptual artist, instrument inventor, wizard, wilderness advocate, poet, philosopher, and permaculturalist working in the grey areas between science, magic and art. David's most recent publication is in the anthology Roots and Routes, Vernon Press (2020). A digital edition of Darkness is the Stone you Cannot Polish came out in the March 2021 issue 10 of Blazing Stadium.

Fortuna Sawahata (She, Her) is a Reclaiming and F(a)eri(e) witch, writer, and artist living in a busy harbor city in the Netherlands. She seeks out and honours the Wild in self, others, and in the Nature that creeps through urban sidewalks and blooms brightly.

SusanneRae is Australian born of anglo-celtic heritage. SusanneRae uses she/they pronouns, activism has been a thread woven into their life since early years. Speaking for rivers and trees over decades in a myriad of circumstances SusanneRae is an active member of the Australian Reclaiming community, teaching regularly and co-creating seasonal rituals.

Additional Resources

Starhawk
  "The Earth Path"
  "Dreaming the Dark"
  "Webs of Power"
  "The Spiral Dance"

"Direct Action: A Historical Novel" by Luke Hauser, https://directaction.org/

"Pagan Portals: Reclaiming Witchcraft" by Irisanya Moon

"Elements of Magic: Reclaiming Earth, Air, Fire, Water & Spirit" by Jane Meredith and Gede Parma

Other books in the *Earth Spirit* series

The Circle of Life is Broken

An Eco-Spiritual Philosophy of the Climate Crisis
Brendan Myers
978-1-78904-977-0 (Paperback)
978-1-78904-978-7 (ebook)

Saving Mother Ocean

We all need to help save the seas!
Steve Andrews
978-1-78904-965-7 (Paperback)
978-1-78904-966-4 (ebook)

MOON
BOOKS

PAGANISM & SHAMANISM

What is Paganism? A religion, a spirituality, an alternative belief system, nature worship? You can find support for all these definitions (and many more) in dictionaries, encyclopaedias, and text books of religion, but subscribe to any one and the truth will evade you. Above all Paganism is a creative pursuit, an encounter with reality, an exploration of meaning and an expression of the soul. Druids, Heathens, Wiccans and others, all contribute their insights and literary riches to the Pagan tradition. Moon Books invites you to begin or to deepen your own encounter, right here, right now.

If you have enjoyed this book, why not tell other readers by posting a review on your preferred book site.

Recent bestsellers from Moon Books are:

Journey to the Dark Goddess
How to Return to Your Soul
Jane Meredith
Discover the powerful secrets of the Dark Goddess and
transform your depression, grief and pain into healing
and integration.
Paperback: 978-1-84694-677-6 ebook: 978-1-78099-223-5

Shamanic Reiki
Expanded Ways of Working with Universal Life Force Energy
Llyn Roberts, Robert Levy
Shamanism and Reiki are each powerful ways of healing; together,
their power multiplies. *Shamanic Reiki* introduces techniques to
help healers and Reiki practitioners tap ancient healing wisdom.
Paperback: 978-1-84694-037-8 ebook: 978-1-84694-650-9

Pagan Portals – The Awen Alone
Walking the Path of the Solitary Druid
Joanna van der Hoeven
An introductory guide for the solitary Druid, *The Awen Alone* will
accompany you as you explore, and seek out your own place
within the natural world.
Paperback: 978-1-78279-547-6 ebook: 978-1-78279-546-9

A Kitchen Witch's World of Magical Herbs & Plants
Rachel Patterson
A journey into the magical world of herbs and plants, filled with
magical uses, folklore, history and practical magic. By popular
writer, blogger and kitchen witch, Tansy Firedragon.
Paperback: 978-1-78279-621-3 ebook: 978-1-78279-620-6

Medicine for the Soul
The Complete Book of Shamanic Healing
Ross Heaven
All you will ever need to know about shamanic healing and how to become your own shaman...
Paperback: 978-1-78099-419-2 ebook: 978-1-78099-420-8

Shaman Pathways – The Druid Shaman
Exploring the Celtic Otherworld
Danu Forest
A practical guide to Celtic shamanism with exercises and techniques as well as traditional lore for exploring the Celtic Otherworld.
Paperback: 978-1-78099-615-8 ebook: 978-1-78099-616-5

Traditional Witchcraft for the Woods and Forests
A Witch's Guide to the Woodland with Guided Meditations and Pathworking
Mélusine Draco
A Witch's guide to walking alone in the woods, with guided meditations and pathworking.
Paperback: 978-1-84694-803-9 ebook: 978-1-84694-804-6

Wild Earth, Wild Soul
A Manual for an Ecstatic Culture
Bill Pfeiffer
Imagine a nature-based culture so alive and so connected, spreading like wildfire. This book is the first flame...
Paperback: 978-1-78099-187-0 ebook: 978-1-78099-188-7

Naming the Goddess
Trevor Greenfield
Naming the Goddess is written by over eighty adherents and scholars of Goddess and Goddess Spirituality.
Paperback: 978-1-78279-476-9 ebook: 978-1-78279-475-2

Shapeshifting into Higher Consciousness
Heal and Transform Yourself and Our World with Ancient Shamanic and Modern Methods
Llyn Roberts
Ancient and modern methods that you can use every day to transform yourself and make a positive difference in the world.
Paperback: 978-1-84694-843-5 ebook: 978-1-84694-844-2

Readers of ebooks can buy or view any of these bestsellers by clicking on the live link in the title. Most titles are published in paperback and as an ebook. Paperbacks are available in traditional bookshops. Both print and ebook formats are available online.

Find more titles and sign up to our readers' newsletter at
http://www.johnhuntpublishing.com/paganism
Follow us on Facebook at https://www.facebook.com/MoonBooks
and Twitter at https://twitter.com/MoonBooksJHP